Famous
Car Factories

Famous
Car Factories

BENGT ASON HOLM
MORGAN

Motorbooks International
Publishers & Wholesalers ®

Famous Car Factories – Morgan has been originated, designed and produced by AB Nordbok, Gothenburg, Sweden.

Editor–in–chief and designer: Bengt Ason Holm
Editor: Jon van Leuven
Special photography: Bengt Ason Holm

Typeset by Citat, Sweden
Reproduction by Offset–kopio, Finland
Printed by Bræmer Tryk, Denmark
Library of Congress Cataloging-in-Publication Data
ISBN 0-87938-558-8

Picture credit list

Cover Graham Harrison. Pages 3–5 Bengt Ason Holm, 12–13 National Motor Museum, 14–15 Morgan Motors, 16–23 National Motor Museum, 24–25 Peter Roberts/Neill Bruce Collection, 26 National Motor Museum, 28 The Motor Cycle, 29 Peter Roberts/Neill Bruce Collection, 30–33 National Motor Museum, 34–36 Peter Roberts/Neill Bruce Collection, 37–49 National Motor Museum, 50–53 Neill Bruce, 57–119 Bengt Ason Holm, 120–121 National Motor Museum, 122–123 Bengt Ason Holm.

Contents

INTRODUCTION

Morgan Motors Company Limited is one of the most unusual car factories in the world. To be sure, it's not the most famous, and millions of common people have never even heard the name. Say Rolls-Royce and everybody thinks "the best car in the world". Say Ferrari and they sigh, "the fastest car in the world". Say Porsche and they're confident: it comes from Germany.

But the Morgan factory is living history with a unique handicraft tradition dating back to 1909. It builds what has often been described as "The Last of the Real Sport Cars". But how can any sensible person today accept the absence of comfort and styling?! Well, Morgan enthusiasts can stand anything. They can even wait up to eight years for delivery of a construction with its roots in the Thirties. But honestly speaking, what is comfort and styling today?

If you should open your motoring magazine today and read the following about the new Japanese 16-valve Turbo 4WD GTi, you wouldn't believe your eyes. These lines comes from The Autocar in the early Fifties: "You must get used to being jolted hard over every bump in a way that would not have escaped unfavourable comments even before the last war." Still today, some of the one-eyed motoring magazines seems to be without the knowledge that the Morgans gives a lot of performance and sheer fun of driving.

But this is a part of the Morgan image, and people have made their pilgrimage to the Morgan Factory for years in order to see how such magnificent cars are produced. The present book is dedicated to all of them, as well as to the unlucky many who haven't had a chance to get there.

Although not a Morgan owner myself, I have greatly enjoyed working on this book. It has never been my intention to make a complete Morgan history, neither a complete description of how they are built, but I hope the text and pictures will be some match for the Morgan myth.

In conclusion I want to address my warm thanks to Peter and Charles Morgan, who made this project possible. My thoughts also go to the friendly, gifted individuals whom I met at the factory. Without them, there would be no Morgans today.

Bengt Ason Holm

How it all began

Automobile history is full of clever and ingenious persons, but most of them have left the scene without much attention, and not all can be found in the history books. Alongside names like Karl Benz, Henry Ford, Ettore Bugatti, W.O. Bentley and Herbert Austin, here is another one to remember – Henry Frederick Stanley Morgan.

Known as H.F.S. to Morgan enthusiasts, he was born in 1884 at Stoke Lacey in Hertfordshire. His father was the Rev. Prebendary H.G. Morgan, a man also to be involved in the early history of Morgan, as we shall see.

ARTIST OR ENGINEER?

H.F.S. was educated at Stone House in Broadstairs, Marlborough College and at Crystal Palace Engineering College. He was obviously very talented, not only in engineering but also in art. Our Morgan fans may well thank the powers above that he didn't choose art as his main occupation! We might have seen a great artist, but the reasons for reading about him in these pages would be non-existent.

At the age of 18, H.F.S. went to the Great Western Railway Works in Swindon. He became a pupil, and soon one of the favourites, of Chief Engineer William Dean. Other famous apprentices at the Works were, in fact, Henry Royce and W.O. Bentley.

After seven years, H.F.S. decided to leave the Works. Although Dean tried hard to persuade him to stay, he was quite determined – he wanted to start a garage in Malvern Link. Besides being the local agent for Wolseley and Darracq, he also ran a successful bus line between Malvern Link and Wells, later also from Malvern to Gloucester.

THE FIRST MORGAN IS BORN

In 1908 he bought a seven-horsepower Peugeot twin cylinder engine in order to build a motorcycle. But for some reason (perhaps because he liked bicycles) he decided to make a three-wheeler. Another wise decision from our point of view!

The Peugeot engine was built into a very light tubular chassis. It is interesting to notice that, whereas a decade later the other ex-Great Western Railway Works apprentice, W.O. Bentley, constructed a large car which eventually grew to locomotive-like proportions, H.F.S. chose the opposite approach. Both were extremely successful.

The first Morgan was built at the Malvern College workshop, where H.F.S. was assisted by Stephenson-Peach, son of the famous steam locomotive pioneer George Stephenson. This workshop had all the necessary machinery for such construction, and in 1909 the car was finished.

This rare picture probably shows H.S.F. Morgan with the very first prototype built at the Malvern College. It is slightly modified, compared with a contemporary shot from 1909, which shows Mr Stephenson-Peach at the tiller. Here, the three-wheeler has side panels, a simple luggage rack, and the silencers now parallel and facing forwards.

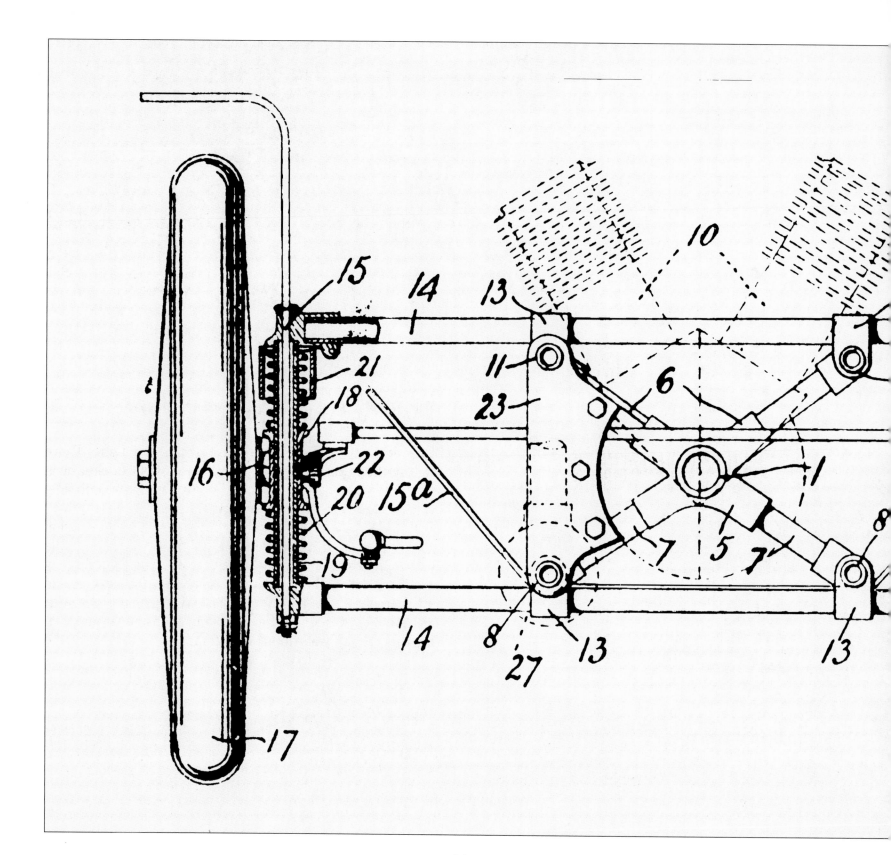

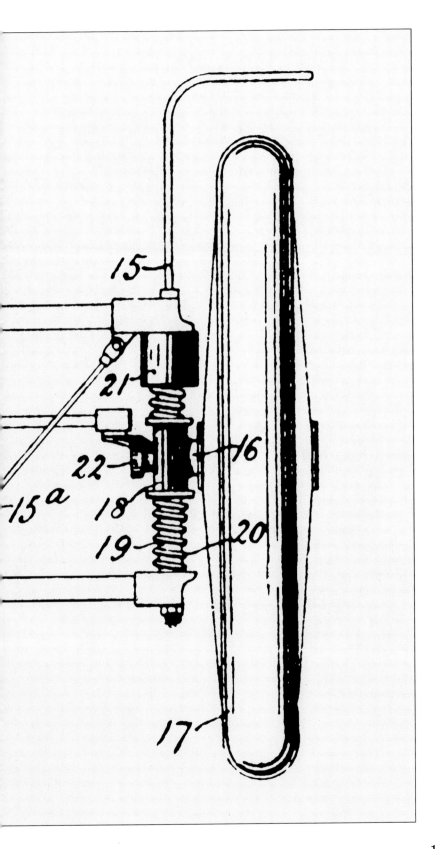

THE FAMOUS FRONT SUSPENSION

The first Morgan was extremely small and light. There was no bodywork and it had only one small bucket seat. Steering was by means of a tiller on the right-hand side, and the petrol tank lay between the driver and the engine.

But the most striking feature was the front suspension (see illustration), which was independent – probably one of the first ever made. The Frenchman Sizaire-Naudin may have been the first to use it in 1908, but his cars became past history already in 1921, while Morgans are still with us. Indeed the same suspension, more or less, is supporting them today. Talk about evolution...

This drawing is a part of the original Patent designs, and shows the famous front suspension. The construction has remained the same, more or less, over the years; and what other company could claim to have used the same suspension since 1908? Today, the same system is used in all Morgans, including the Plus 8 – a car with a 200-bhp engine and acceleration, 0-100, better than a Ferrari Testarossa.

The system features a vertically mounted coil spring on a sliding axle pin, not unlike the system used on the Lancia Lambda, but by no means a copy.

DEMANDING FRIENDS AND AN UNDERSTANDING FATHER

H.F.S. was not really aware of what he had done, but the news of his little three-wheeler spread rapidly. Soon his friends asked him for a copy of the car, something which he hadn't thought about. Building for business was not what he had intended: it was more like a hobby-horse that he had created.

But yielding to pressure, he decided to go commercial – and in 1910, with the help of £3,000 which his ever-sympathetic father lent him, the Morgan Motor Company Ltd was founded. The sum was sufficient to buy a suitable building, tools and materials. Some capital was also raised by advance fees for each car ordered.

Thus the production of Morgans began, and we are fortunate to see no end of it. On the contrary, the business is prospering as never before.

This is probably the original three-wheeler exhibited at the Olympia Motor Show in 1910. The engine is a 8-hp JAP V-twin, and on the right-hand side of the seat is the steering tiller, whilst the controls on the left side are gear change, accelerator and engine retard and advance mechanisms.

SHOWS AND COMPETITIONS

In late 1910, H.F.S. took two cars to the Olympia Motor Cycle Show. They were fitted with a 961-cc JAP V2 engine, a make which was later to appear on many famous English motorcycles.

The reception was quite cool, but he soon understood why. He had to build a two-seater, as the single-seater was too sporty for the public. He went back to Malvern Link and, in 1911, had the first two-seater ready.

In the meantime orders were coming in. It is noteworthy that one of the first agencies for Morgan three-wheelers was an obscure company in Knightsbridge, London. The company's name was Harrods, the now world-famous department store.

But the absolutely best way to obtain maximum attention was to enter competitions. By the end of 1913, Morgans had won hill climbs, trial races, and Grand Prix races for cyclecars – and had broken a record at Brooklands with nearly 60 mph.

Again an appropriate word was success, and the news flashed through all important motoring magazines, helping to boost sales. That year, the cheapest two-seater Morgan

The record run at Brooklands in 1912 with H.S.F. in the seat. Amongst the people surrounding the car are Preb. H.G. Morgan (in top hat) and the timekeeper A.V. Ebblewhite. In one hour, a distance of 59 miles and 1,120 yards was covered. The picture above is the same that covered "The Cyclecar" of December 4. At right is a unique, although somewhat blurred, action shot from the rough Brookland banking.

could be bought for 85 guineas. The price for a "Bullnose" Morris Oxford was then £175 (and a pound, of course, was only one shilling less than a guinea).

Shown here is the chassis erecting shop in the old factory at Worcester Road, which was abandoned in 1919. On the wooden trestles are far more chassis than nowadays, and we can also see the very simple but effective construction of the chassis.

It is built of tubular steel and strengthened by the central prop-shaft tunnel. On the rear end is the gearbox casing and temporarily hanging loose on the prop shaft tunnel is the rear wheel support. The chassis in the right row have been fitted with the quarter-elliptic rear springs. In the corner are a couple of belt-driven machines, and in the centre stands H.S.F. Morgan.

*Entering competition of all kinds was from the very beginning an
important part of the H.F.S. strategy. He was convinced that success on
the race courses meant better business, and he was right. Victories
boosted the sales.*

*One of the most important in those early days was W.G. McMinnie's
win in the 1913 French Grand Prix for cyclecars, or "voiturettes" as the
French preferred to call them. This class originated from France, which
did not like to always be beaten by German and Italian monster-cars
with engine capacities up to 24 litres.*

*McMinnie finished first, 2 minutes and 45 seconds ahead of Bourbeau
in a Bédélia and the English magazines were full of enthusiasm. Listen
to this quote from the "Pall Mall Gazette": "No one who is not on the
inside of the racing game as it is played in France can realise the
magnitude of the undertaking when a foreign competitor sets out to beat
the French cracks at their own game – not that they do not play fairly,
but they start with a heavy handicap in their favour for they are used to
driving at high speeds on their own roads. They practically drive at
racing speeds all the time they are on open highways and their corner-
work is a thing to be admired."*

*At the wheel is McMinnie and the passenger is the mechanic Frank
Thomas, who had also prepared "The Jabberwock". The picture was
originally published in the "The Motor Cycling Magazine".*

22

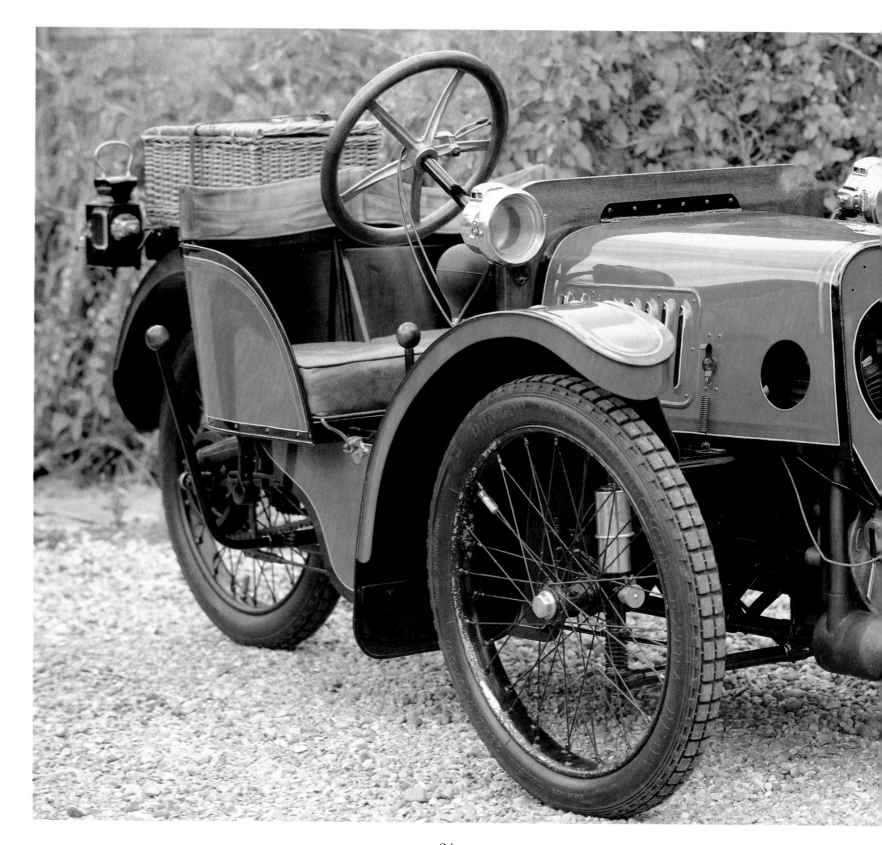

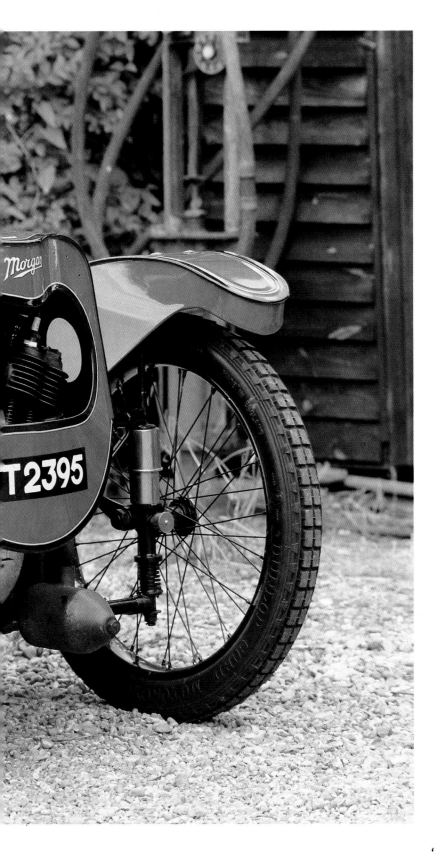

WAR MEANT BUSINESS

By the outbreak of World War I, Morgan Motors made nearly 1,000 cars per year, and the profit in 1914 was just over £10,000. Three different Grand Prix single-seaters as well as two-seaters for road use were produced.

The war helped business as the Government ordered large quantities of munitions. While H.F.S. was something of a pacifist, he couldn't object to such orders. They made good capital, even though the purpose was horrid.

Government contracts actually kept Morgan going throughout the war years, and a small number of cars was produced. Interestingly, they even had time to produce a four-wheeler prototype in 1915. More fantastic is the fact that the very same car was unearthed some years ago. But

An early production Morgan, a two-seater from 1913 with an air-cooled JAP engine of 954-cc capacity. The gearbox had two forward gears but no reverse, and gear-change was made with the lever just in front of the rear wheel. The top speed was around 45 mph and the price 85 guineas.

this model did not go into production and 22 years were to pass before a four-wheeler left the factory. When the war was over, it didn't take long until car production was in full swing once more, and in 1919 it was time to move to another place. The works at Worcester Road had become too small for the ever-increasing demand for small, inexpensive vehicles.

PICKERSLEIGH ROAD

At the end of 1919 the new factory was completed, and in early 1923 all production, except for the machine shop, had moved to the new address – Pickersleigh Road – where it still is. A curious detail is that, in 1919, the factory produced 20 cars per week. Today the number is 10!

The company was in a very healthy state and H.F.S. did not need to borrow any money for the new factory. It all

To the left is an early picture, probably around 1920, of the chassis erecting shop at Pickersleigh Road. Note the roof construction, which can also be seen in the modern pictures later in this book. To the right is a French licence-built Morgan – a Darmont.

came from his own resources, and there was enough left to buy him a Rolls-Royce and a new house. Henry Frederick Stanley Morgan was beginning to enjoy the fruits of his labours.

The factory now had a yearly output of nearly 2,500 cars. In addition, Morgans were made under licence in France, between 1920 and 1930, by an agent named Darmont in Courbevoie. The Darmont was also very successful in hill climbs and trials. By the end of 1924, a total of nearly 40,000 cars had been produced on both sides of the English Channel.

"Make it a "Morgan Holiday"

Why stay at home and envy your friends who get out every holiday, every week-end? You can get away to the seaside too—as inexpensively, as comfortably, as surely, as satisfactorily —by Morgan. The Morgan Runabout costs much less than a car, yet gives the same performance. Its tax is only £4, its petrol consumption 50 m p.g., its speed 60 m.p.h., there are only three tyres to maintain, and the Morgan is simple to handle, easy to understand.

This ad, from a copy of the MotorCycle, shows a 1926 Family model. The price was ú116 and the picture clearly shows that Morgan now also was aiming for the non-sporting market. Below is a Standard which was sold for ú95.
If you compare the two pictures you will notice the difference in size; the artist has managed to make the Family model look very large with its dwarf-sized lady driver.

A VARIETY OF MODELS

In the middle of the 1920s, there was a choice of several models, starting with the cheapest model: Standard, the first series-produced four-seater. Next came the Family model, which could be had with a water-cooled JAP-engine; then the Grand Prix, the Aero with Blackburn engine, and the Super Sports Aero.

Later the Aero had a choice of three different engines: either a 980-cc side-valve JAP, a 1,078-cc overhead-valve Anzani, or a 1,096-cc overhead-valve JAP, the latter with a top speed of about 72 mph. The Super Sports Model was the fastest of them all, reaching 80 mph.

DARK CLOUDS ON THE HORIZON

The period between 1920 and 1930 saw four serious threats to the Morgan Company. The first came when the post-war boom was over, and the second with the introduction of the Austin Seven. Third, of course, was the Great Depression at the end of the decade, and fourth were the taxation changes in 1935.

In 1923 the post-war party was over, and a lot of small cyclecar manufacturers were fighting for their lives. The situation became really bad when Herbert Austin, in 1923, introduced his little Austin Seven with the intention to make "motoring possible for the millions" who had long been waiting for a small and cheap car, big enough to carry the whole family with some dignity. The Austin Seven was the answer.

The response was overwhelming. In 1922 the following

Racing was still an important way of marketing Morgans and, in this magnificent shot from around 1922/24, we see D. Hawkes in his Anzani-engined record-breaker. Note the absence of front-wheel brakes and the diameter of the unsilenced exhaust pipe. It must have produced a terrific sound.

lines were to be found in The Light Car: "a decent car for the man who, at present, can only afford a motorcycle and sidecar, and yet has the ambition to become a motorist". This was indeed going to be a threat to the Morgan Company!

And what measures did H.F.S. take to meet this challenge? Yes, he cut prices – but more importantly, he cut the production in order to reduce the stock of unsold cars. This turned out to be a very sensible decision, and matched his intention of creating a very special car. Thus he found his own special niche in the market, and the Morgan image was born.

At the end of the 1920s, the Depression hit Europe and America, and many manufacturers had to give up. Among the more famous was W.O. Bentley, who had to sell out to Rolls-Royce.

THE EARLY COMPETITORS

Of all the threats to the Morgan Company during the Twenties and Thirties, one was particularly aggravating. For the first time, Morgan faced competition; and first out with a comparable three-wheeler was B.S.A., who in 1929

introduced a two-cylinder model, followed in 1933 by a four-cylinder model. But B.S.A. had to stop production in 1936.

What had gone wrong? Well, it's never an easy job to follow in somebody's footsteps, and the B.S.A. three-wheelers had one disadvantage – they were too sophisticated for their customers. B.S.A. continued with four-wheelers until 1940, but gave up car production after the war. At the beginning of the Sixties, the motorcycle factory tested a three-wheeler called Ladybird, but nothing came of it.

The next big challenger was Raleigh from Nottingham. In 1933, they introduced a four-seated three-wheeler with a 742-cc four-cylinder engine. It had a three-speed gearbox and shaft drive. The model name was Safety Seven, and about 1,000 were built before production ended in 1935.

To the right are two of Morgan's three-wheeled rivals at the beginning of the Thirties, a B.S.A and a Raleigh (insert). The B.S.A. came in two versions, a 1,100-cc 2-cylinder model priced at £100 and a 1,075-cc 4-cylinder, watercooled model at £125. Both had front-wheel drive. Production started in 1929 and ceased in 1936.

The Raleigh, which was called the Safety Seven, had a 742-cc 2-cylinder V-engine, 3-speed gearbox and shaft drive. Its constructor was T.L. Williams who later founded the Reliant Motor Company, still in existence at Tamworth. The production of three-wheelers lasted between 1933 and 1936.

The 1928 Blackburn-engined Morgan Super Sports in racing trim as used at Brooklands in 1929. The production version had a 40-bhp, 1,096-cc JAP engine with 3-speed gearbox. Top speed was around 80 mph and the price in 1930 was £145.

THE FIRST FOUR-WHEELER

By the mid-1930s it was quite obvious that three-wheelers, in technical terms, were at their peak. The last model, denoted F, had a 1,172-cc four-cylinder engine, conventional frame with Z-shaped side-members, three-speed gearbox and self-starter.

There was nothing more to add, but the most alarming thing was the sales record. In 1934, 659 Morgans were sold – yet by the end of 1936, only 137 left the factory. Henry Stanley Frederick Morgan just had to do something!

And he did. To everyone's surprise, a four-wheeler was introduced – not at the Olympia Motor Show, but as a headline in *The Light Car and Cyclecar*. The Morgan 4-4 was born.

While the prototype had been fitted with the same Ford Ten engine used in the three-wheeled F, the production model came with a 1,112-cc Coventry-Climax "ioe" (inlet over exhaust valve). The output was 34 bhp at 4,500 rpm. The front suspension was the old one, although somewhat modified and reinforced. At the rear were a live axle, semi-elliptic springs and hydraulic shock-absorbers.

In the mid-Thirties, it was quite obvious that the three-wheeler sales were insufficient to keep Morgan Motors going. In order to save the company, the first 4-wheeler was presented in December 1935. Seen here (right) is a 4-4 from 1936 with H.S.F. Morgan at the wheel.
The 4-4 was no immediate success in the conservative Morgan camp – many thought it was not sporty enough and went for a M.G. instead. But with a little racing success, the sales rose and by the end of the Thirties, 887 cars had been sold.

Above is the last three-wheeled model, the Morgan F4, which had a 1172-cc Ford Ten engine. Suspension and power train were the same as earlier, but the chassis members were made of Z-shaped steel sections, as on the four-wheeled cars. The F4 was produced into the early Fifties.

NO IMMEDIATE SUCCESS

At first, people were a little suspicious because this was not one of the expected products. Although it had a Morgan badge, it also had "four" wheels, which were one too many.

But the 4-4 was well received by the Press, and H.F.S. (now in cooperation with his son Peter, born in 1919) immediately entered rallies and trials with never-ending good fortune, and the public slowly changed its mind. At the outbreak of World War II, Morgan Motors had sold 887 four-wheelers.

One decision which helped to increase the sales figures was the introduction of the 1,267-cc overhead-valve Standard engine in 1939. It produced 39 bhp at 4,800 rpm

Above at right is Peter Morgan battling a morass at Beardshaw's Bog in the 1936 High Peak Trial. Below is a picture from the 1936 Torquay Rally, and it is most certainly H.S.F. at the helm this time. Note that the registration number is the same as on the car above.

On the opposite page is a situation from the 1938 Tourist Trophy. The model is a 4-4 factory racer which also entered Le Mans in both 1938 and 1939. The car had a 1,098-cc Climax engine and was later sold in a limited edition to the public. The man in the chequered cap seems to be a little thoughtful, and one wonders what the young boy is musing about — maybe a future racing career.

CHANGING TIMES AT MORGAN

Around 1936, there occurred a series of events which were important to the Morgan Company in one way or another, and one of them could certainly have made this story shorter.

In October 1936, a fire broke out in the factory. By sheer luck, it was restricted to the body shop. Take a look at the pictures in this book (not much has changed since 1936) and you can imagine what might have happened. The body shop was quickly rebuilt, and the only result of this incident was some delay in deliveries.

The next event came in November of the same year, when H.F.S.' father and long-time supporter, George Morgan, died. Whether or not because of that, H.F.S. slowly began to change his life and paid less attention to the daily routine at the factory. A new managing director, George Goodall, was appointed and he also contributed to the Morgan image with several competition successes.

This is probably the prototype Morgan 4-4 Drophead Coupé seen passing a ford during a trial event in 1938. The car behind is a HRG.

THE SECOND WORLD WAR

War proved to be profitable as usual, provided that you didn't have to go to the battlefield. When it was over, the Morgan Company was ready to enter production again, with money left over from the Government contracts.

But restarting the production line this time was not as easy as after the Great War. The reason was simply that, during the last war, part of the factory had been leased out to other companies, who couldn't be thrown out at once. Those companies were the Standard Motor Company and Flight Refueling Ltd. An interesting note is that, during one period, a complete Handley Page bomber was to be found in the Carpenters' Shop.

Another problem was the return of the workers, which took much longer than expected. In 1945 only a few cars were assembled. Among those who came back from service was P.H.G. Morgan who, in 1947, joined the company as Draughtsman and Developing Engineer.

On the bright side of the war business was all the machinery which the Government had installed, and the fact that the Morgan factory was located in a part of England which did not suffer much from heavy bombing during the early part of the war. While many others went out of business, these machines kept the factory going and H.F.S. was later able to buy some of them at a very good price.

EXPORT OR DIE

A new threat to many companies in England was the Government demand for heavily increased export. This new situation led to a restriction in steel supply, if one did not respond to the demand. For small companies like Morgan, that meant life or death. Thus Morgan was forced to get dealers abroad, and in 1948 the first dealerships were established in France and America.

By the beginning of the Fifties, Morgan was more or less in the hands of the American market – and even worse, the Morgan image began to fade. The cars were "hopelessly outdated", compared with such cars as the Jaguar XK120, the Triumph TR2 and the M.G. MGA, all

A Morgan 4-4 four-seater from 1948. This model was in all respects the same as that made before the war, and production ended in 1950. In the background is another famous British car – a Morris Minor.

introduced between 1953 and 1955. But history was going to prove otherwise.

In 1951 the last three-wheeler and in 1950 the last 4-4 were made. A new model was introduced, the Plus Four, with a 2,088-cc Standard Vanguard engine. Later on, this model had engines from the Triumph TR2, TR3 and TR4 – and by 1954 all Morgans had the sloping radiator cowl, which has become famous and is still in use today. The fastest Plus Four was the Super Sports, built between 1961 and 1968.

The 4/4 (now called 4-4) was back in 1955, now with a 1,172-cc Ford Anglia engine, subsequently with engines from Ford Classic and Cortina.

The competition continued after the war and this picture is from the London Rally in September 1952. The model is a slightly modified 4-4 from about 1946/47, and it seems to be a little chilly. One of the crew members is wearing a RAF bomber jacket over his trenchcoat.

Also note the cars in the background, which are typically English bread-and-butter vehicles from the period. HBT 32 is a Hillman Minx and the car with the roof-rack is a Vauxhall Fourteen of around 1938/39.

Two Morgan Plus Fours. (Left) A misty shot from the early Fifties and, below, a picture from the 1952 RAC Rally.

KUY 474

A

As mentioned, the American market was the most important one for the Morgan Company. When this market collapsed at the beginning of the Sixties, Morgan was in serious trouble. But with the help of Peter Morgan, who went to America, and the American enthusiasts, the market recovered. Peter Morgan returned to England and for a period of two years he worked hard on expanding the Morgan market to other parts of the world. He also ordered a production cut to one car per week, a decision made before by his father.

THE PLUS FOUR PLUS –
BOTH A FLOP AND A HIT

Since the war, the English market had been unsuccessful. But in 1964, Morgan did something which astonished the motoring press and the public. The Plus Four Plus was introduced.

It was completely different from all other Morgan cars. With a sleek and handsome glass-fibre body, which bore some resemblance to the Jaguar XK120, it surprised the

world. Could really Morgan change? Yes, indeed!

After 26 cars and two body-shells, the production was stopped. Yet the interest it created in the traditionally shaped Morgan was enormous. And when Morgan won its class at Le Mans in 1962, people started to realize that there was something special about the cars from Malvern Link.

As seen before, headlines was very important for the people at Pickersleigh Road – but not only when competing in races. Here come some more interesting pictures.

A. The famous Plus Four Plus from 1965. Only 26 were made but they created enormous interest: not for themselves but for the traditionally built Morgans. The Plus Four Plus helped to strengthen the growing Morgan myth. Under the body made by British Resin Products Ltd was the usual Morgan chassis. B. A Plus Four in the Silverstone 6-Hour Relay. C. A Plus Four in a 1954 M.C.C. meeting at Silverstone. D. Eastbourne Rally 1954. This is an interesting special driven by R.K.N. Clarkson. Behind the Ferrari - inspired body is a Plus Four.

E. A great moment for Morgan was the class win in the 1962 Le Mans (see picture on page 117), but already in 1930 Miss Lynda Fawcett and Mr White also came in 13th overall. Unfortunately they didn't win their class. F. Chris Lawrence continued to race Morgans successfully in the Sixties and here is his very special Plus Four-based SLR Special racing coupé from 1964.

B

E

C

F

D

A 1972 Morgan 4/4.

POWERED BY FIAT

Can this be true, Morgan addicts asked themselves, when it was announced in 1981 that the 4/4 was going to be fitted with a Fiat engine? In fact, it was a result of the important German market, whose emission regulations did not approve the current Ford engine.

The Fiat unit was a 1,585-cc overhead-valve engine, earlier used in the Fiat 124 Sport and the 131. The output was 97 bhp at 6,000 rpm. But despite being a good engine, it was not British. According to rumour, when a Ford executive learned that his recently ordered Morgan would have a Fiat engine, he promptly arranged delivery of the new Sierra engine. From 1981 there was a choice of both engine types.

MORGAN PLUS EIGHT

A very expensive and important step was taken in 1966, when the board decided to build the Plus Eight. This step was taken after the supply of Triumph TR engines had ceased and Morgan needed a replacement. The Rover V8 engine was selected as a result of a visit to Malvern Link by Peter Wilks, a director of Rover.

Wilks discreetly asked whether Morgan would be interested in a Rover take-over, but Peter Morgan resisted. If he hadn't, we would probably have seen a Honda-engined Morgan today or, worst of all, no Morgan at all.

The Plus Eight was an immediate sensation, with overwhelming Press response. Once again, Morgan had proved the the clocks were not paralyzed in Pickersleigh Road.

The Plus Eight was also well-received in America, but when Rover withdrew from the American market in the early Seventies, Morgan also had to go. Nevertheless, a very determined American, Bill Fink, managed to make the impossible possible – and in 1976, Morgan was back on the American market. And all due to using propane instead of petrol. Similar problems occurred in many countries, but today Morgan is back on most markets and the Company thrives as always.

This is probably the most important Morgan model produced after World War II – the Plus Eight. Here is a 1982 model fitted with the ex-Buick, Rover V8 of 3,532 cc. Output was 192 bhp, later raised to a full 200. In 1990, the model was fitted with a catalytic converter but still managed to show acceleration figures in a class with the Ferrari Testarossa.

THE TROUBLESHOOTER

In May 1990, the Morgan Company once again was challenged by outside forces. Not by governments and safety-approval problems, this time the attack came from the venerable British Broadcasting Corporation. In a BBC 2 series called "The Troubleshooter", various businessmen were invited to analyze the difficulties of small companies and suggest solutions. The Morgan Company was approached and, according to Charles Morgan, once a mass-media man himself at ITN, "Of course we were happy to cooperate."

The man chosen for this particular program was Sir John Harvey Jones, former chairman of ICI. He arrived in a chauffeur-drive limousine, in fact a Volvo (forgive me for my Swedish origin), and walked around the factory just as we shall do later in this book.

Sir John spooked. "They should double the production, put up the prices to pay for new investment, and build a new plant — but their pride seems to be in manufacturing from the furthest-back state they can, buying the most basic material. I am surprised they don't start with the tree itself."

The Morgan people were taken aback, but reacted very quickly. When the contents of the program were revealed later, one person at Morgan remarked: "You would think that someone coming to tell a car company how to run a business would at least be able to drive himself" (*Daily Telegraph*, 3 May 1990). And they sent out a press release.

THE PRIDE OF MORGAN

When this story comes to the notice of Morgan fans, I think they will react in the same way as when the Plus-Four-Plus was introduced. The traditional Morgan will get even more attention and Sir John will have to eat his hat.

The day after the BBC program, one dealer in London had orders for ten Morgans, and in the space of 3 months, 401 orders were received. That makes the waiting list even longer. Let us now enter the factory and see how this old-fashioned car is produced.

At right is the famous Morgan Press Release of May 1990, caused by the attack of Sir John Harvey-Jones in BBC's program "The Troubleshooter". For the first time, Morgan Motors officially defended their philosophy and way of building cars.

"Troubleshooter"
BBC 2, May 1990, 9:00 PM

As many of you will have heard, the Morgan Motor Company is due to be featured in this series presented by Sir John Harvey Jones. The program discusses the Company and ways in which we might increase our production to satisfy our long waiting list.

It is Sir John's view that we should double our production in a short time-scale, paying for this by increasing the price of the car and investing in an expensive new plant. His methods would result in making many changes to the traditional way the Morgan is built.

We disagree strongly with his solution, and believe the Morgan policy of gradual and carefully considered change will enable us to maintain the car's qualities, and unique appeal, and thereby ensure its survival for the foreseeable future. The Company is indisputably successful. We believe our car is fairly priced and we, as an independent Company, have no hungry shareholders demanding immediate returns to our long detriment.

New technology is constantly under review. It is only now that it is becoming more suitable, and available, to a quality manufacturing process such as our own, rather than to mass-production operations. The installation of a "state of the art" paint and powder coating operation confirms our desire to improve processes and make possible an increase in levels of production.

The car itself is constantly benefiting from improvements to its specification. At present a fully catalysed 3.9-litre Plus Eight is undergoing type approval and certification. This takes us to a clean emission standard in excess of standards proposed in Europe. With its blistering accelereation provided by its horsepower and torque, this car will be a truly "green" real sports car.

Whilst many improvements are carried out under the skin, we do not want to change the craftsmanship that goes into the car. Hand-finished panels and wood frames, with the craftsman constantly checking his quality standards, are all attributes of the Morgan that will not be superseded by modern technology. Because the car is built by people, not machines, each car has a "soul" and each customer can verify this for himself by seeing his particular car being built. To change this would, in our view, be a step backwards.

So the Morgan will continue to adhere to H.F.S. and Peter Morgan's principles of design — a simple lightweight sports car, with excellent power to weight ratio, that gives unrivalled responsiveness and driving feel. This is what some mass producers are now attempting to engineer into their products.

Our factory will continue to conserve its traditions of craftsmanship and quality. The Directors and work force will remain open to change and will adopt new technology to improve the car and the level of production at the factory. Sir John's criticisms have been noted, but his solutions are unworthy of us.

Yours sincerely,
Morgan Motor Co. Ltd.

Charles Morgan
Director

Morgan today

It is now time to enter the factory and have a look at today's production. In the case of Morgan this sounds a bit pretentious, because today's production is the same as yesterday's. What you will see within these walls has its roots in the beginning of our century, and the production methods have not changed much over the years.

Of all the classic car factories in the world, Morgan is unique. Almost nothing has changed here, while for example Daimler-Benz A.G. in Germany – the oldest surviving (at the moment) car manufacturer – is making technically advanced cars in modern factories. And Rolls-Royce, another great producer in this series of books, was born in 1904 but turns out up-to-date luxury cars, partly more or less handmade.

The process going on at Morgan is living history: not unparalleled in itself, as the skills exist in many restoration shops, but unique in that new cars are built by the same methods which were used during the 1920s. Someone has aptly remarked, "Morgan recoils from doctrines fashioned to the changing hour". (Dennis May, *Automobile Quarterly*)

Over the years I have made several visits to the Morgan Factory, all with the feeling of touring a "Mecca". Yet my best experience was in 1986, when I entered the factory yard during a heavy rainstorm. The windscreen wipers on my new rent-a-car Austin Montego had seized – seemingly an act of Lucas, maliciously said to be the man who invented darkness. Not fair, but an expression of the common attitude towards British quality established in the 1960s, when not even the wildest British-car enthusiast abroad could defend the Union Jack. In that climate, Morgan Motors Ltd saw a long line of English cars pass into extinction.

Anyhow, the wipers were on strike and I was muttering something like "Don't they ever learn their lesson?" when I saw a familiar sight through the streams of water. Two men were rolling a half-completed Morgan down the yard. Suddenly I forgot all about British quality and thought: "Ah, they still have their mobile assembly line..." I had come to the Morgan Factory!

What makes a Morgan so special? The way it is built or for what it is? An "old-fashioned" sports car with charm and performance, handmade by devoted craftsmen in a manner far away from modern production. Ask a Morgan owner why he owns a Morgan and why he is making a pilgrimage to Pickersleigh Road. There you have the answer!

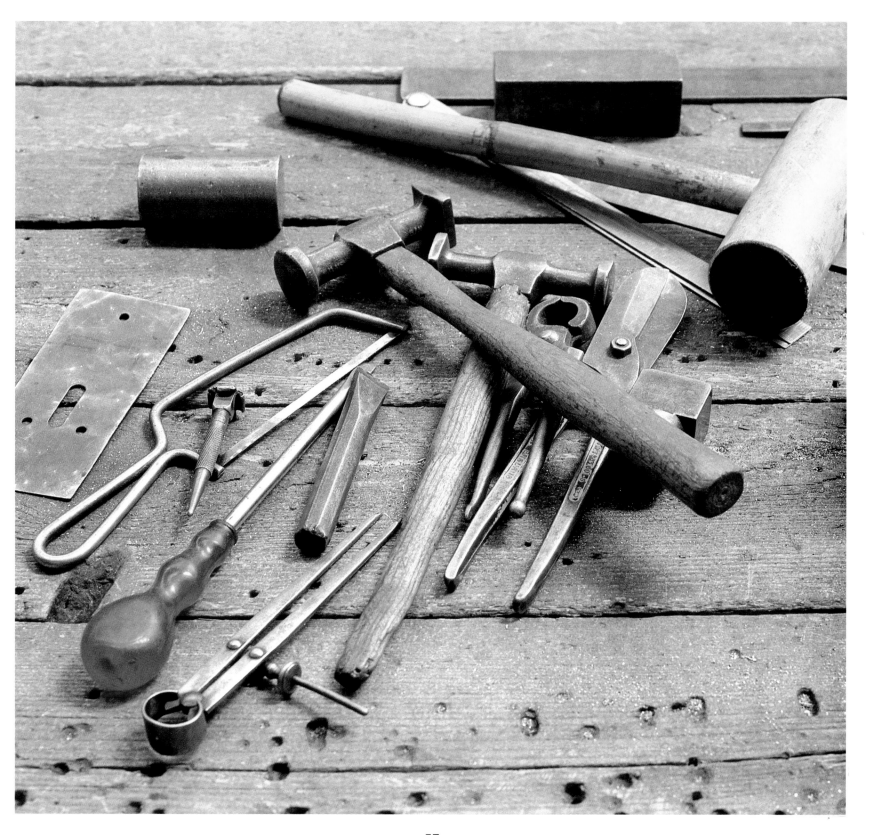

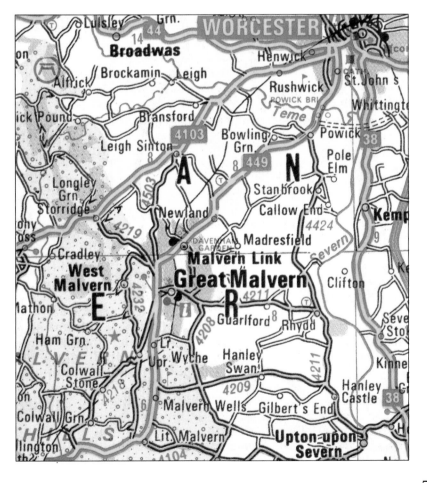

NOT QUITE AS EXPECTED

Normally, you may guess, they start the assembly at one end of the factory and finish it off at the other. But that's not the order of the day at Morgan. Here, cars are moved about in a complicated pattern, which requires careful planning. Otherwise the result would be literal chaos.

But let us commence from the outset – in the Chassis Erecting Shop (E). (The capital letters in parentheses refer to the location on the factory plan, at the beginning of this chapter.)

This is the place where Morgans begin life — which is perhaps not the full truth, because already on stage are some vital parts that have been manufactured both inside

To the left is a map which shows where the Morgan Motor Company is situated. It is in Malvern Link, close to Great Malvern which is about 11 miles south of Worcester. From London to Worcester is about 106 miles in a west-north-westerly direction.

To the right are some outside views.

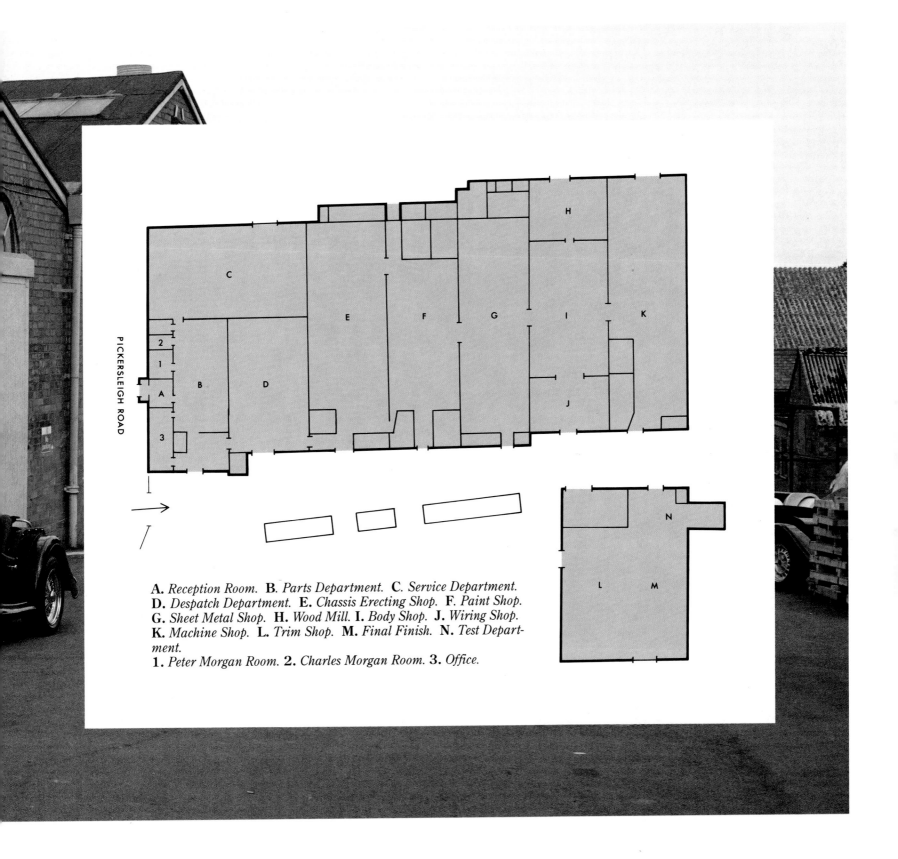

PICKERSLEIGH ROAD

A. *Reception Room.* **B.** *Parts Department.* **C.** *Service Department.*
D. *Despatch Department.* **E.** *Chassis Erecting Shop.* **F.** *Paint Shop.*
G. *Sheet Metal Shop.* **H.** *Wood Mill.* **I.** *Body Shop.* **J.** *Wiring Shop.*
K. *Machine Shop.* **L.** *Trim Shop.* **M.** *Final Finish.* **N.** *Test Department.*
1. *Peter Morgan Room.* **2.** *Charles Morgan Room.* **3.** *Office.*

and outside the Morgan factory. First of all, there are the actual chassis, made by the Parkfield & Thompson in Wolverhamton. Every ten days a lorry arrives with about 20 chassis. Secondly there are the engines, which come from Rover and Ford, also in sufficient quantity to avoid production stops. Finally, there is a batch of rims and tyres, again from beyond the walls.

NUMBERS ARE MAGIC

The bare chassis frames are delivered into the hall on a wheel-cart named H.M.S. Ark Royal, which used to be H.M.S. Hermes before it was rechristened. The change of name was a tribute to the aircraft carrier *Ark Royal* and her successful operations during the Falkland War.

Wooden trestles are placed on the floor, and two men lift the frames onto them. Nearby are laid items such as

Tea time in the Chassis Erecting Shop. This picture was taken in May 1990 and if you count the chassis, you will notice that there are ten on the line, not nine as the rule always has been. The chassis to the right is not part of the assembly line.

springs, prop shafts, front stub axles with disc brakes, shock absorbers, pedal sets, brake pipes and handbrake cables. After that, assembly begins and four men deal with the work in rotation so as to avoid monotony. There are never more than nine chassis in production at once (since this manuscript was written, the number is raised to ten).

Why only nine chassis, you may ask – why not ten, fifteen or even twenty? The demand for Morgan cars around the world is absolutely unbelievable, and in some countries the waiting-list is over ten years. The answer you get is wonderful. "Nine are enough – it's a nice figure, and we've always made nine. So why stress, when we're happy and make a good profit" That sounds very British indeed.

The "underslung" chassis – which means that it hangs under the rear axle – is a simple construction with two rather deep, Z-shaped side members and several cross members for stiffening. All parts are painted black, and at an extra cost you can have the chassis rustproofed by the Terotex Process or galvanized.

The front wheels are individually sprung, with two vertically mounted coil springs on sliding axle pins and double-acting tubular shock absorbers. This arrangement resembles the type used on the famous Lancia Lambda in the 1920s, but is scarcely a loan from the Italian company.

A Salisbury rear axle with springs ready to be mounted. This axle is used for all cars; only the ratios are different. The Plus Eight has 3.31:1, the Plus Four 3.73:1 and the Four/Four 4.1:1. This specimen is for a Plus Eight.

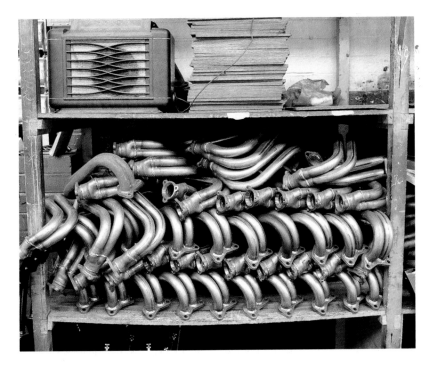

A batch of exhaust pipes. The factory always keeps a buffer stock of parts to avoid shortages which could cause delays and thus create chaos in the cramped spaces available in the different manufacturing shops.

It was, in fact, already used on the Morgan three-wheelers as early as 1909. Nor is the chassis design a youngster, having been created in the mid-1930s. At the rear is a live Salisbury axle with drum brakes, which hangs in semi-elliptical springs and Armstrong lever-type hydraulic dampers. The specifications for the axle, springs and shock absorbers may vary a little, but are basically the same for all models.

THE MORGAN RANGE IN 1990

Before we go far into details, it is worthwhile to survey the different models produced.

The top model is the Plus Eight, with an aluminium V8 engine of 3.9 litres capacity, generating 200 bhp. Next on the scale is the Plus Four, with a Rover 16-valve four of 1994 cc and 138 bhp. Finally there is the Four/Four, with the four-cylinder Ford CVH engine of 1597 cc and 98 bhp. All four-cylinder models come either as two-seaters or as four-seaters.

And now back to the production. As stated earlier, all the chassis assembly is mostly made by hand; only when fitting the engines is a muscle-powered gantry used. Once all parts are in place, including a wooden tankboard underneath the fuel tank, the wheels are added and the chassis is lowered to the ground.

There are four different types of wheels available. But as standard, the Plus Eight is delivered with cast aluminium rims, and the Plus Four and the Plus Four with stove enamelled wire wheels. As an option, chromium-plated wire wheels can be supplied. These can also be had with stainless steel spokes.

At last we have nine completed chassis with drivelines on the floor, and it's time for the long shuffle through the factory. In a couple of minutes, two men – with the help of a movable hydraulic jack – shift the chassis aside. A queue forms, waiting for transfer to the body shop. One week has gone, and the process has to start again with nine bare frames.

Screws, bolts, nuts, washers and spring washers. A lot of these bits and pieces are required to keep a Morgan together. To the right are some brake-line connections and the "insider" will immediately recognise all the different pieces. For the rest of us, they are just beautiful to behold.

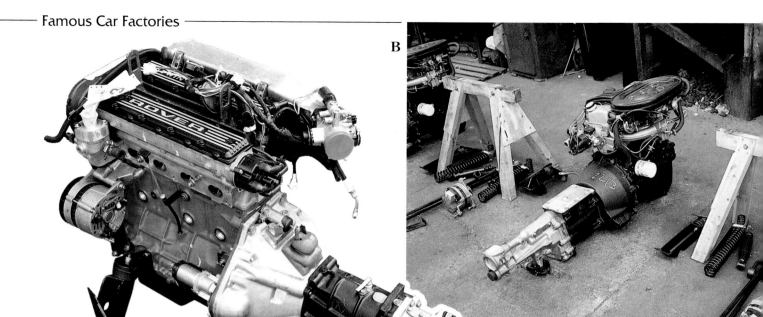

They used to do this operation on a Friday, but when I visited the factory in March 1990, it happened on a Thursday. Who said that things weren't changing? Anyhow, the important thing is that the operation should run on schedule, to avoid traffic jams in the crowded premises. A special "removal squad" is called together via the internal communication system, and when the message has reached the men involved, the chassis are slowly rolled down to the body shop.

A collage from the Chassis Erecting Shop. **A.** *The 4-cylinder, 16-valve 2-litre engine for the Plus Four also comes from Rover. Output is 138 bhp at 6,000 rpm.* **B.** *The smallest engine in the program is the Ford engine supplied to the Four/Four. Capacity is 1,597 cc and output 95 bhp at 5,750 rpm.* **C.** *Big brother in the engine family is the mighty Rover V8. Recently the output of this 3,528-cc engine was raised from 192 to 200 bhp, 0-60 in 5.8 seconds. Believe it or not!*

D

F

G

E

This part shows some details of the chassis. **D.** *A batch of Salisbury rear axles (see also picture, page 64). The mouldings for the brake drums and hubs are made outside the house but finished in the the machine shop.* **E.** *Rear springs. These have seven leaves and are destined for the Plus Four or the Four/Four. The Plus Eight has six leaves.* **F.** *As mentioned on page 66 there are four different types of wheels and this chromium wire wheel can be had as an extra.* **G.** *This week's batch of chassis is completed and waiting to be rolled down to the Body Shop.*

THE BUILD TICKET

As a prelude to the body shop, a few words must be said about the "Build Ticket". A document made in advance of production, it accompanies all cars from the beginning. On this piece of paper, everybody in the production line can see which model is involved, whether any extras are ordered, and where the car will be delivered. Here is an example of a "Build Ticket":

Agents name	Wendel Motor
Model	Plus-8
Chassis number	R9423
Engine number	10A45812
Rear axle number	A85-274
Colour	Green
Upholstery	Black
Speedometer	Km/h
Extras	Left-hand drive
	Luggage rack
	Locking petrol cap
	Door handles
	Cuprisol
	Quartz clock
	Seat belts
	Aluminium body and wings
	Badge bar
	Undersealing

By checking this list, it is possible to pre-order any parts required, which is very important if you should be short of storage space. To make this clear to everyone, a small announcement on the wall says: "To ensure that the thing you want is always in stock, please order replacements while it's getting low – they don't appear by magic."

COACHBUILDING – THE MORGAN BODY

The body shop is divided into three parts: the Sheet Metal Shop (G), the Wood Mill (H) and the Body Shop (I). The first two are the heart of this extraordinary production unit, and here is the final destination of all the Morgan enthusiasts who make their pilgrimage to Pickersleigh Road in Malvern Link. The scene is, once more, a bit of living history where men and skills join together in an exceptional handicraft, unique in the automobile world today.

The basic material for making the sub frames is seasoned ash. Seasoned means that the timber has to be stored for many years prior to use. The storage makes the ash dry, hard and strong. The material is perfect for this

purpose, and not only because it's strong: it is also easily worked, but still more importantly, it is light.

When the timber is ready for use, it is carried into the Wood Mill (H) and manufactured into diverse pieces for the sub and door frames. The mill also manufactures floor-

71

boards and dashboards and altogether there are 72 pieces in the two-seater body and 116 in the four-seater. Some countries, for example, demand extra woodwork for the four-seater in order to fit seat-belts in the rear compartment. Well, even Morgan has to adapt itself.

UNWANTED MEMORIES FROM THE GREAT WAR

If the production methods are old-fashioned, so is the machinery. Some of it is more than sixty years old but still working perfectly. The threat to it has been not the tooth of time, but the very timber being worked. Some years ago, the factory used a batch of timber from Belgium, which had grown near a battlefield of World War I. What has that to do with the timber? Well, suddenly the milling machines

There is a Rembrandt-like atmosphere in this scene from the Wood Mill, and if you look carefully, you will discover that the man at the band-saw has given more than his skill in the art of manufacturing the different parts for the Morgan wooden sub frame.

were damaged for some unknown reason, and when investigated, it turned out that some of the timber was full of shell-splinters. It is up to your own fantasy to think that you may have such memories built into your particular car – provided, of course, that you are a Morgan owner!

GONE IS THE SMELL OF FISH

The work in the body shop is the same now as at the beginning of this century, and only a few techniques have changed. One of them – a very smelly one – was the use of fish glue, a nasty liquid that has been abandoned in favour of modern synthetic cold glue, which gives a much better and stronger joint. But speaking as a puritan (and that's easy to do when you aren't forced to work with it), the smell of fish glue is something to be nostalgic about.

Among the most complicated jobs in the body shop is the production of the wheel arches. These are made of laminated ash and shaped in a heated cupboard with the aid of wooden blocks and clamps. This is a tricky job which takes time, and the process must go on constantly to avoid production stops.

THE WOODEN BIRDCAGE

When the sub frames are finished, they are fitted to a chassis, or else stored in a corner of the body shop. The sight of a batch of sub frames can create the image of a giant surrealistic birdcage – and a birdcage made by craftsmen.

After the sub frames are fitted to the chassis, the doors can be fitted, and naturally all doors are individually adjusted to fit the sub frame. As a result, all Morgans are different – and if you have to replace something, the same adjustments have to be done. That's a part of the Morgan charm, which the Morgan addict takes for granted.

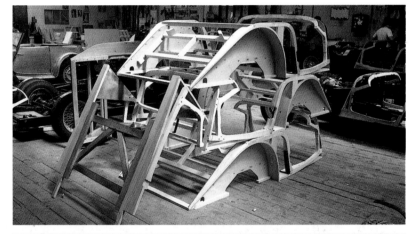

(Left) Another view from the Wood Mill. Only your own imagination sets the limit for what you could expect to find on those shelves. (Right) A pile of finished sub frames. Since the frames are all individually made by different workers, the doors are not yet put in place as they must also be individually mounted and adjusted. When the frames are finished they are dipped for 24 hours in a tank of cuprinol.

ROTTING BODIES: A PROBLEM SOLVED WITH CUPRISOL

Before fitting a sub frame to the chassis, it is dipped for a minimum of three hours in a tank with cuprisol; sometimes it is left overnight. This is a quite recent innovation, which replaced black paint. It was not long ago that soaking with cuprisol was an optional extra, but this process became standard five years ago when the demand for better quality arose.

As a matter of fact, Peter Morgan told me, by far the best advertising is to have as many Morgans as possible on the road. "That helps us to sell even more cars," he observed, "The owners are the cars best salesmen."

More pictures from the Body Shop. On page 76 we can see the different parts for a door, and below a couple of finished door frames with the brass hinges mounted. On the opposite page, two- and four-seater bodies are being assembled. There are 72 parts in a two-seater and 116 in a four-seater.

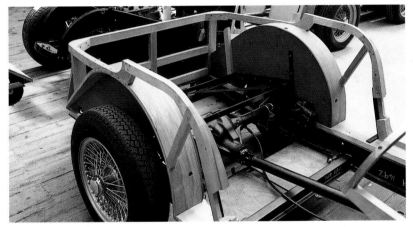

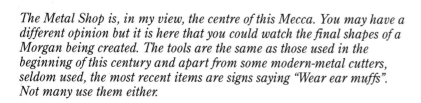

*The Metal Shop is, in my view, the centre of this Mecca. You may have a
different opinion but it is here that you could watch the final shapes of a
Morgan being created. The tools are the same as those used in the
beginning of this century and apart from some modern-metal cutters,
seldom used, the most recent items are signs saying "Wear ear muffs".
Not many use them either.*

A CHOICE OF STEEL OR ALUMINIUM

The next chamber in our "Mecca" is the sheet metal shop, devoted to the arts of cutting, bending, beating and soldering. Here the sub frame panels, as well as the bonnet, are shaped with an adeptness that makes you stand watching for hours, quietly contemplating your own lack of skill. Written on the wall is an appropriate sentence: "If you think we do this out of the goodness of our hearts – think again!" The words "think again" have been crossed out and replaced with "we do"...

The noise hurts your ears, but the signs saying "wear ear muffs" go unnoticed. The use of ear-savers is apparently not accepted, and the tools are as ancient as ever, even though I saw some modern metal-cutters. Everybody seems to prefer the old type of hand-powered tin-snips, as it gives a more accurate feeling in difficult working positions.

Normally the bodies are made from sheet metal, except for the rear three-quarter panel and the rear panel which are of aluminium. But as an extra option, the body and wings can be obtained in aluminium. Panel thicknesses

are: metal front and valance, 20 gauge steel; scuttle and doors, 21 gauge steel, rear three-quarter panel and rear panel, 18 gauge aluminium; and all other sheet metal components, 22 gauge steel.

The only parts not made by Morgan are the wings and the cowl, which comes from the Manchester company of Eva Brothers. The reason for this is simple. The production requires huge rollers in order to bend the sheet metal to the right curvature, and Eva Brothers are specialists in making wings for lorries and other commercial vehicles. The wings united with the running boards are impressive when they stand upright against a wall, as high as a tall man.

The wings are fitted when all body panels are screwed and tin-tacked to the sub frame. Even though the wings look fine, they are adjusted individually to fit each particular car.

Six pictures from the Metal Shop. On page 80 a scuttle and a door come to life, and on page 81 other body parts are being produced. As always, they are a bit different from each other.

NO BONNETS FOR SCRAP

Production of the bonnet is a difficult operation which requires large muscle-powered machinery and craftsmanship. This item is made from a sheet of metal, measuring 84 x 44 inches before being cut into two halves. Then each half is bent to the right curvature and the louvres are pressed out, one by one, with an old fly-press. No fixtures are used; only some pencil lines on the metal provide the information about where to put the press. If a single louvre is out of line, the bonnet is scrapped – but I was told that this seldom happens.

As with all other parts, the bonnet is individually fitted to the car and is not interchangeable with others.

The producing of a bonnet is one of the most tricky operations in the Metal Shop, and the louvre pressing is a one-man show. The only help he gets is muscle-power from his assistant. The success of the operation depends on whether the bonnet is in the right position. Then he shouts: "Press". When the bonnet is ready, it requires careful adjustment. Worth mentioning is that if you have to fit a new bonnet to your car, this one too requires personal adjustment.

TO THE PAINT SHOP WITH BETSY

Now the car is ready for the paint shop (F). The removal squad is called in and the car is wheeled straight through a doorway into the paint shop.

When you enter the paint shop, you finally recognize something from "the new age": two modern paint boxes stand on each side of the shop. But that's all, and for an outsider, the overall impression is of half-organized chaos.

On the floor are cars in all stages of work. The average time spent in the paint shop is over two weeks, and as many as forty cars can be found there at the same time. The wheels have now been removed and special "slave wheels" has been fitted with thick layers of old paint, giving the spokes twice their normal thickness.

When the cars are going to be painted they can't retain their original wheels. Instead special slave wheels are mounted, whose spokes, with the years, became thicker and thicker. Admit it – they are beautiful!

SMOOTH AS A BABY'S BOTTOM

The painting process starts by cleaning the bare metal with a soft acid, strong enough to remove all traces of dirt and grease. Then all welding joints are covered with a filler and filed down, an operation made much easier today, thanks to modern welding techniques.

Afterwards a very thin coat of colour is applied, which unmercifully shows all dents and scratches. All irregularities are filled with a stopper, the colour is rubbed down and a primer is sprayed on. This sequence goes on until the surface is as smooth as a baby's bottom, and altogether tree or four coats are applied and rubbed down. All this rubbing is a back-breaking job, but essential – no top coat can hide a bad undercoat.

When the surface has been inspected and given a go-ahead, the car is rolled into the Spraybake owen, where the first coat of colour comes on. Sometimes the car goes

The painting process is a matter of being patient. If the filler work and all the rubbing-down are badly done, no top coat in the world can hide them. As the top coat is very thin, the body must be rubbed down, smooth as a baby's bottom.

back for further treatment because, indeed, the top coat can't hide anything. But if every square inch is OK, the colour is rubbed down, a new coat of colour is applied and the process is repeated. Normally the car gets four or five coats, but if the paint has a thin depth of pigment, a couple of more coats are required.

CHOOSE ANY COLOUR YOU WANT

The colours available today are black, connaught green, cream, indigo blue, ivory, red and royal ivory. But any ICI colour is available, even dual-tone paint. The latter, however, is not so popular to deal with, as it requires a lot more work. A special colour paintwork costs about £60 extra, Metallic £230 and Dual tones £310.

Finally the car gets a black coat inside the body. This is brushed on, in order to avoid masking the body for protection. Then it's time to move again.

This is also a piece of art. Fresh-painted bonnets for the big toy cars. Choose any colour you want; a special colour paintwork will cost you only £185.

THE LUCAS CONNECTION

The painted car is rolled down into the Wiring Shop (J), a cramped space, wall to wall with the body shop. Some years ago it occupied an even smaller area, next to the chassis erecting shop.

Here the electrical system is fitted. Many parts still comes from Lucas, but the lights are from Marelli and the instruments from VDO.

Holes are drilled, rubber grommets are fitted, and the wiring harness is laid out to all the different stations where a current is needed. If any extras are ordered, for instance a radio or an electrical clock, attention is paid to them. After wiring, the lamps are fitted, and finally the battery.

Some other jobs are also done in the wiring shop. The exhaust system – with or without catalyst – are fitted as well as the bumpers. Finally the Morgan badge is put on the radiator cowl!

The Wiring Shop.

THE SMELL OF LEATHER IS IN THE AIR

After electrification the car is once again taken outside, and this time pushed across the yard, to a building just opposite the wiring shop. We are now in the last assembly department, which hosts the Trim Shop (L), the Final Finish (M) and the Test Department (N).

In the trim shop – a pleasantly silent spot compared with some of the noisy places we have visited hitherto – all interior trim, floor mats, seats and hoods are fitted. The material used is leather from the legendary Connolly Brothers, and though there are some jokes about Joseph Lucas, there are definitely none about the Connollys. Leather from this company is used all over the world by quality-minded car manufacturers.

Cutting leather is another of those skills that have roots in the old coachbuilding traditions. The feeling and aroma of leather are astonishing. You often see people just caressing a leather seat with something special in their eyes. And leather seats also age with dignity, becoming more beautiful each year.

If the "build ticket" has been an important document so far, here is the place where it really matters. Connolly leather is very expensive, and the factory can't afford to keep a large stock of all different colours that might be required but black and brown are always available.

THE WHINING SINGER MACHINES

Interior work starts with the trim panels, which are cut to the right pattern in the sawmill. They are then covered with PVC or leather (90 %), and tacked into place with nails covered by a hide band.

The trim panels are an easy job to tackle, but the leather seats are much more complicated. Once all parts are cut out with the help of patterns, the ladies take over. Although I saw a few girls in the body shop, this is the real place to find them. I don't know whether they do a better job, but for some reason history has decreed that they are better at sewing. And it has decided that men do the cutting. (At this point a memory returns from one of my visits to the Ferrari factory, where I was introduced to the master cutter, who had left a prosperous business in a famous Milanese dress-fashion emporium in order to work for Ferrari. The girls who actually did the job were never introduced to me!)

Anyhow, here they do it fantastically well and the finished product is a delight to behold. Best of all, of course, would be to sit in the Connolly seats, switch the ignition key, shift into first gear, and take off into the hills over Malvern...

The master cutter is often the king in the Trim Shop, but what about the girls who bring it all together? Without their particular skill, there would be no seats and panels. The leather used is, of course, from Connolly Brothers in Wimbledon. To the right is an interior shot from the Trim Shop.

THE ORIENTAL ENTHUSIAST

At times during my walk through the factory I saw him: the man from Japan in his flawless dark suit, carrying a Hasselblad camera on a tripod, taking an endless stream of pictures. Fascinating, I thought; those Japanese are always snapping away.

And now he was standing in front of me, shooting the trim shop. It turned out to be a member of the Morgan Sports Car Club of Japan, Mr Takao Kanemitsu from Tokyo, who was visiting "Mecca". We had a conversation about Morgan and the fact that he was using a Swedish camera – while I, who live in Gothenburg, the home town of Hasselblad, used a Nikon. It all ended with me promising to send him a copy of this book in due course. My best regards to Mr Kanemitsu.

We are now close to the final preparation, and the interior is completed with all sorts of details like carpets, dashboards, windscreens and hoods. In a couple of days, the car will be ready for its first test drive. It is now about 8 to 10 weeks since the production started.

LONG GONE IS THE MAHOGANY DASHBOARD

After the Japanese encounter, it's time for the last bits and pieces to be fitted. Our journey is approaching its conclusion. There is certainly more to see, but at this stage one might feel that the party is soon over, and look for a chance to leave such an interesting place. So there is no difficulty in underestimating how much remains to be done on the car. A windscreen is fitted, the seat rails are screwed onto the floorboards, and carpets are fitted. When these jobs are complete, the fitting of the hood is on the programme. The hood is made after a fixed pattern, but the trim buttons are positioned individually.

One of the last parts to be fitted is the dashboard, and unfortunately it's no longer in solid mahogany. Instead we must stick to a rather disconcerting, padded dashboard with modern-looking switches. Those were the days, when you could enjoy the lovely sight of a beautifully veneered walnut dash! Yet the odd thing is that, under the Morgan padded dash, there is still a wooden panel and on some markets, a dashboard with a thin layer of burr walnut is allowed.

THE GRAND FINALE – A STEERING WHEEL

After a three-month tour the car is ready to be delivered. Not to the customer, but to the test driver – and now comes a symbolic moment. The final steering wheel is fitted (the other one was just for dirty hands), and the car tanks are filled with water, oil and petrol.

The engine is fired up, the ignition is adjusted, and a short test-drive is performed. After that, further adjustments are made and, before being delivered to the despatch department, the car is run for about 20 miles. As a complement to the road test, there is a "rolling road" where the brakes and transmission can be tested, as well as the CO (carbon monoxide) readings.

Sometimes, but rarely, a car fails to pass the last test and is sent back for further attention. The majority of cars do pass, and after testing they are undersealed and embark on their last trip in the factory yard.

On most markets, the walnut dashboards are no longer allowed, and we have to accept those ugly padded boards. But there is a wooden board behind the padding, although not in walnut. So please enjoy the view on the opposite page!

OWLS ARE WATCHING

In the Despatch Department (D), the cars are stored until delivered to the dealers, or occasionally to a happy owner who prefers to collect his darling in person. In the meantime, gnomes in the form of two static owls watch over the cars, in order to frighten any birds that might choose the despatch department as a resort and drop their "visiting cards" on the gleaming products.

The walls are cramped with all kinds of Automobilia related to Morgan. These include posters, photos, greetings from abroad, and a large handmade flag. Its motif is of course a Morgan, which rests in an ocean of flowers, and on top of the bonnet lies a man embracing the car. The text is short and precise: "My heart belongs to Morgan".

Otherwise the most exciting discovery was to find a Ferrari stuck in behind the Morgans. "It belongs to the boss but he never uses it." That was no surprise, since the light metallic 365 GT was covered in a layer of dust.

The two most important "inmates" in the Despatch Department are the gnome owls who scare the life out of visiting sparrows. The light metallic blue car in the background belongs to Peter Morgan. It is a FERRARI!

THE MACHINE SHOP

We have now been to all parts of the factory which the cars pass during their three-month tour, but there are some more areas worth visiting, and one of the most important is the Machine Shop (K).

This is a dim abode and the equipment looks outdated. Some pieces are well over fifty years old, and the forge seems to be from the turn of the century. But the machinery is extremely reliable, and most men prefer the old lathes to a modern one installed a few years ago.

Here, a broad assortment of parts is machined and forged from castings produced outside the factory. They may be, for instance, brake drums, discs, hubs, stub axles, kingpins and bushes as well as suspension parts, slats for the radiator grille, petrol tanks and gearbox bell housings. The most spectacular product in the machine shop is actually not a car part, but a selection of incredible steel chairs

The lighting conditions in the Machine Shop are not the best for the people who work there, or for taking pictures – and it would have been a shame to use a flash. You just had to hold your breath and hope they wouldn't move too much. This particular shop is soon to be modernised.

A

– individually produced like all Morgans. They are spread all over the place and provide a good place to sit down and have your afternoon tea.

The machine shop is soon to be rebuilt, according to Charles Morgan. One can only hope that it, too, is done the "Morgan way". Cross your fingers!

B

A collection of pictures from the Machine Shop.
A. *Slightly rusted brake drums waiting to be put in a lathe.* **B.** *Brake drum receiving the final touch in the lathe.* **C.** *Wheel hub getting the same attention.*

C

D. *The famous front suspension starts its life in the Machine Shop.* **E.** *Turning is nice to look at, especially when the cooling liquid is splashed over the hot metal.*

A. *A selection of home-made Morgan chairs.* **B.** *Steering knuckles.*
C. *The control panel on one of the veteran lathes.* **D.** *Veteran and brake drums.* **E.** *A batch of wheel hubs awaiting delivery.*

108

D

E

THE SPARES DEPARTMENT

Many years ago it was not unusual that Morgans deteriorated to a stage where they had to be scrapped. This was due to the small business with spare parts. But today the situation has changed dramatically, and scrapping a Morgan is virtually unheard of.

Increasing popularity means that the spare-parts busi-

ness has raised its volume far above the traditional level. Almost any part can now be supplied, and sometimes in quantities to a single customer that may suggest the entire car is being rebuilt.

It is not only dealers and private customers who are supplied. The factory itself needs hundreds of parts to build a car. Until quite recently, spare-part numbers were not used, but this has changed. Today all shelves in the parts department (B) are marked with a number and a colour, although there is still no parts list available, and such a thing as a workshop manual doesn't exist?

When asking how far back you could go in requesting parts, I was told that they could supply almost anything since the 1950s. The staff showed me a an old front-suspension frame which someone had sent to the factory. It was slightly different from today's construction, but they were going to modify it a new one on behalf of the customer. That's what I call service.

The Parts Department is one of the key areas in the factory. First of all, they supply all Morgan dealers and owners with spare parts; but more importantly, they also service the "assembly line" so that there is no shortage during production.

THE SERVICE DEPARTMENT

This department (C), which looks more like an ordinary English restoration shop, is situated at the back of the factory. In it we witness "what could happen" to a Morgan when not treated with love. The floor is covered with cars in all manner of condition. New cars, competition cars and cars in a state which leaves you wondering if they'll ever be finished.

Under a pile of worn-out tyres I found one sample which must have been there for ages. It was dismantled, and the only thing that seemed to have been done was the fitting of a pair of new shock absorbers. Perhaps the owner is no longer with us — or has he run out of money? At all events, this place is a far cry from the service department at your local Ford or Volvo dealer. No white coats in sight, thank you.

The Service Department looks more like an ordinary English restoration shop for Vintage cars than what we are used to seeing at our local Ford dealer. Some of the cars have been here for years and will probably stay for a while.

THE RECEPTION ROOM

Your first encounter with Morgan Motors will probably be the Reception Room (A). If you expect to find a hall with a marble floor, stainless-steel cabinets, spotlights and a portrait of Peter Morgan beaming down from the wall, you'll be disappointed. This is a simple room with an entrance from the street. The walls are covered with paintings, charts with racing results (up to 1913) and a glass cabinet with diverse Morgan regalia. Here you can buy a ladies' purse, a scarf, a tankard, a pocket-flask, a pocket knife, a lapel badge and stickers. Just name it and it's there with the Morgan badge on it. There is also a selection of Morgan literature and sales brochures. On top of the desk is a Guest Book with names from all over the world.

An average of 10 visitors a day comes to the factory and they have always been welcome. Let us hope it will remain that way.

The Reception Room is the first place you will see, provided that you enter from Pickersleigh Road, and the room is extremely simple with its white panelled walls. Here are no marble, bronze statues or fancy decorations – just a few pictures and an old victory chart, which was unfinished already in 1919. On the desk is the Guest Book

Peter Morgan in his office. The wall is covered with memorable moments and the centre picture shows one of the greatest when Richard Shepherd-Barron takes the flag in the 1962 Le Mans, winning his class. They covered a distance of 2,256 km in 24 hours and finished 13th overall. To the right of Peter Morgan is a diploma from the Morgan Owners Group of Sweden.

The pictures on this spread were taken in 1972. They are interesting to study. Compare them with the modern one. What has changed – or is it the same.

FRY
472D

A batch of Plus Four's leaving the factory in 1966.